THE PLANT-BASED MUCUS CLEANSE DIET RECIPE BOOK

Naturally Healing Mucusless Superfoods to Eliminate Mucus-Forming Foods, Detoxify, and Stay Healthy

ALEX BROWER, RD

DEDICATION

To all those on a journey toward better health, may this book empower you with knowledge and inspire you to make choices that nourish your body and mind.

To my patients, colleagues, and loved ones, your support, curiosity, and resilience continue to fuel my passion for holistic wellness.

And to my family, for your unwavering encouragement and belief in my mission—this book is for you.

Alex Brower, RD

COPYRIGHT PAGE

© 2025 by Alex Brower, RD

No part of this book may be copied, stored, or shared in any form - whether electronic, mechanical, photocopied, recorded, or otherwise—without written permission from the copyright holder. Exceptions apply for brief excerpts used in reviews or academic discussions.

Disclaimer

This book is intended for educational purposes only. It is not meant to diagnose, treat, cure, or prevent any disease. Always consult a healthcare professional before making any changes to your diet, exercise, or lifestyle, particularly if you have an existing medical condition.

TABLE OF CONTENTS

DEDICATION 2

COPYRIGHT PAGE 3

TABLE OF CONTENTS 4

MUCUS AND HOW IT AFFECTS YOUR HEALTH .. 1

    When Mucus Becomes a Problem 9

    Symptoms of Excess Mucus Buildup 12

    Common Causes: Diet, Allergies, and Environmental Factors 14

    What You Can Gain From a Mucusless Diet 16

TOP AND WORST FOODS FOR MUCUS CLEANSING 24

    Common Hydration and Herbal Remedies for Mucus Reduction 28

The Worst Offenders: Dairy, Processed Foods, and Sugar 41

How to Identify Mucus-Forming Foods 43

DELICIOUS MUCUSLESS BREAKFAST RECIPES TO TRY 48

1. Mucusless Alkaline Green Smoothie 48

2. Chia Seed Pudding with Berries 49

3. Quinoa Porridge with Cinnamon 50

4. Alkaline Fruit Salad 51

5. Sprouted Buckwheat Granola 52

6. Coconut Yogurt with Flaxseeds 53

7. Avocado Toast on Spelt Bread 54

8. Warm Fig & Date Smoothie 54

9. Sautéed Plantains with Walnuts 55

10. Sweet Potato Pancakes 56

11. Apple-Cinnamon Breakfast Bowl 57

12. Mango-Banana Smoothie Bowl 57

13. Amaranth Porridge with Dates 58

14. Cucumber & Avocado Wrap 59

15. Pineapple-Ginger Detox Juice 59

DELICIOUS MUCUSLESS LUNCH RECIPES TO TRY 61

1. Quinoa & Roasted Veggie Bowl 61

2. Avocado & Cucumber Wrap 62

3. Sweet Potato & Lentil Stew 63

4. Mango & Spinach Salad 64

5. Spaghetti Squash & Pesto 65

6. Chickpea & Avocado Salad 66

7. Baked Plantain with Black Beans 67

8. Roasted Cauliflower & Tahini Dressing 67

9. Stuffed Bell Peppers with Quinoa 68

10. Cucumber & Avocado Gazpacho 69

11. Roasted Eggplant with Tomato Sauce 70

12. Zucchini Noodles with Cashew Cream 71

13. Carrot & Beet Slaw 71

14. Steamed Kale & Garlic Mushrooms 72

15. Pineapple & Avocado Salsa with Quinoa 73

DELICIOUS MUCUSLESS DINNER RECIPES TO TRY 75

1. Roasted Eggplant & Quinoa Bowl 75

2. Zucchini Noodles with Avocado Pesto 76

3. Stuffed Bell Peppers with Lentils 77

4. Cauliflower & Chickpea Curry 78

5. Sweet Potato & Kale Stir-Fry 79

6. Spaghetti Squash & Mushroom Medley 80

7. Broccoli & Almond Stir Fry 81

8. Warm Lentil & Spinach Salad 82

9. Roasted Carrot & Ginger Soup 82

10. Butternut Squash & Quinoa Pilaf 83

11. Cabbage & Avocado Wraps 84

12. Grilled Asparagus & Quinoa Salad 85

13. Baked Cauliflower Steaks 86

14. Roasted Brussels Sprouts & Walnuts 86

15. Steamed Okra & Tomato Salad 87

DELICIOUS MUCUSLESS SNACK AND DESSERT RECIPES TO TRY 89

1. Alkaline Energy Balls 89

2. Cucumber & Avocado Slices 90

3. Mango & Coconut Chia Pudding 91

4. Spiced Roasted Chickpeas 92

5. Watermelon & Mint Salad 92

6. Almond Butter & Banana Bites 93

7. Baked Plantain Chips 94

8. Apple & Walnut Snack 94

9. Carrot & Hummus Sticks 95

10. Pineapple & Coconut Bites 95

11. Zucchini Chips 96

12. Almond & Fig Snack 97

13. Fresh Guacamole & Veggie Sticks 97

14. Cantaloupe & Mint Delight 98

15. Roasted Pumpkin Seeds 99

HEALTHY TIPS FOR CLEARING MUCUS 100

1
MUCUS AND HOW IT AFFECTS YOUR HEALTH

Mucus consists mainly of water and a gel-forming molecule called mucin. The body uses mucus to protect tissues, remove particles, and prevent infections. Mucus is essential for the functioning of many of the body's organs.

A person might think their body only makes mucus in response to illness, allergens, or irritants. However, the body is always producing mucus, which is crucial for the functioning of several organs and the immune system.

Many health issues can lead to a mucus buildup, drawing a person's attention to this key bodily fluid. Most healthy people never notice that they are continually producing and swallowing it.

Where mucus comes from

Mucus is a fluid that the body produces to line moist areas, such as the:

- Eyes
- Mouth
- Nose
- Sinuses
- Lungs
- Throat
- Stomach
- Intestines
- Reproductive Organs

Most people only notice mucus when they are ill or exposed to allergens or irritants in the air. But glands in the areas listed above make mucus continually, secreting around 1 to 2 quarts daily.

Mucus helps with crucial functions, such as:

• Adding moisture to inhaled air

• Preventing moist organs from drying out

• Filtering, trapping, and eliminating inhaled microparticles or microorganisms, such as allergens, dust, smoke, pollution, viruses, bacteria, and fungi

• Protecting the surface tissues from infection

• Maintaining a healthy balance of bacteria in the gastrointestinal tract

Mucus helps trap microorganisms and microparticles on the surface of the lungs. Tiny hair-like appendages called cilia line the lungs and beat in unison, creating a pulse that moves the entrapped particles up and out of the lungs.

Once the particle-filled mucus reaches the back of the throat, it typically moves down the throat without the person noticing.

After traveling down the throat, the mucus reaches the stomach, where it is digested and eliminated from the body in feces or urine. Mucus in the throat can also be coughed up and spit out.

What is mucus made of?

Mucus is mostly water, but it also contains important proteins and sugars. The cells that make mucus also produce molecules that support immune function, which are incorporated into the mucus.

The molecules in mucus include:

- Immune-Modulating Molecules

- Protective molecules

How the body makes mucus

The tissues lining the airways, nose, sinuses, and mouth contain two primary cell types: secretory cells, which release the components of mucus, and ciliated cells. These are covered with tiny hair-like projections called cilia.

Mucus is mostly water and a gel-forming molecule called mucin. Special secretory cells called goblet cells are the predominant producers and releasers of mucin. A goblet cell is shaped like a medieval goblet, and it is not covered with cilia.

Goblet cells and other secretory cells also release a range of proteins, salts, fats, and immune molecules that mix with mucin and are incorporated into mucus.

Submucosal glands, found in the airways, mouth, and gastrointestinal tract, also produce and release mucin and mucus.

Ciliated cells use their tiny projections to move mucus throughout the body. The cilia move in a way that creates a unified pulse, pushing mucus along in waves.

Infections and irritants

When the airways are exposed to irritants, goblet cells and submucosal glands produce extra mucus to clear the airways.

In addition, infections can cause inflammation in airway tissues, which can likewise trigger the submucosal glands to produce more mucus. During an infection, mucus thickens because it fills with immune cells and entrapped foreign particles.

Allergic reactions occur when the immune system responds excessively to a harmless substance. The reaction triggers the release of histamine — a compound that can cause the airway linings to swell and stimulate the submucosal glands to produce more mucus.

Function

What does mucus do?

Mucus has a lot of important jobs, including:

• Blocking germs and harmful particles from getting into your body's tissues.

- Housing antibodies to disable and mark germs for destruction by immune cells.

- Trapping things that could harm you and moving them out of your body.

- Moisturizing your mucous membranes (mucosa) — the parts of your body that open to the outside world.

- Lubricating your mucous membranes. This helps different parts of your body perform different functions. For instance, it helps food move through your digestive tract and provides a way for sperm to get to an egg for fertilization in your reproductive tract (cervical mucus).

What does mucus look like?

Mucus is usually clear, thin and slippery. If you have a respiratory or sinus infection, the mucus coming out of your nose or throat may be thick, sticky and creamy white. Dead cells, germs, tobacco smoke and other substances in your mucus can change its color. Mucus colors include:

- **White, cream-colored or light yellow.** When your mucus gets dense and appears white or creamy, it usually means you're fighting a cold or other viral infection. The color and thickness come from immune cells fighting the infection.

- **Bright yellow or green.** This also is usually a sign of infection. Based on your other symptoms and how long they've gone on, it could mean you have sinusitis, or a bacterial infection in your sinuses.

- **Red or pink.** Blood can make your mucus pink-tinged or streak it with red. You might have blood in your mucus if your nose is dried out or irritated. Small blood vessels in your nose can burst and leak blood.

- **Brown.** Air pollution or smoking can cause brown mucus. It also could be a sign of infection.

- **Black.** This can be something you inhaled, but it can also be a sign of a serious fungal infection.

Mucus color alone won't tell you if you have a specific kind of infection. See a healthcare provider if you have dark-colored mucus — or any other color that concerns you — especially if you have other symptoms, like facial pain or headaches.

What color mucus is healthy?

When you're not sick, mucus is usually clear. Thick mucus that appears creamy, yellow or green could mean you have an infection. You might get a runny nose with large amounts of clear mucus if you have allergies.

When Mucus Becomes a Problem

Having phlegm or mucus doesn't necessarily mean you have something serious. It's how your body removes irritants in your throat and nasal passages.

However, if you cough it out and it doesn't seem to resolve, it may be a sign of an infection or other condition.

Make an appointment with your doctor if you have any of these symptoms:

- Your mucus isn't going away
- Your mucus is getting thicker
- Your mucus is increasing in volume or changing color
- You have a fever
- You have chest pain
- You're experiencing shortness of breath
- You're coughing up blood
- You're wheezing

These signs may indicate more severe illnesses like pneumonia, COPD, the flu, or COVID-19.

Possible complications

If a buildup of mucus is severe or persistent, it can lead to:

- Dehydration

- Postnasal drip

- A sore throat

- Sinus or nasal pain or pressure

- Jaw pain

- A cough

- Lung, nasal, sinus, or throat infections

- Digestive problems

- Weight loss

- Trouble breathing

- Reduced oxygen levels and increased circulating carbon dioxide levels

- Atelectasis, in which the lungs cannot fully expand or collapse

- Respiratory failure
- Heart failure

Symptoms of Excess Mucus Buildup

Excess mucus buildup can leave you feeling sluggish and congested. While mucus is essential for keeping your body lubricated and protected, too much of it can cause a range of uncomfortable symptoms. Here's how to tell if your body is producing more mucus than it should:

Breathing Issues

- Constant coughing or throat clearing

- Stuffy or runny nose that won't go away

- Mucus dripping down the back of your throat (postnasal drip)

- Feeling like you can't take a deep breath or wheezing

- Sinus headaches and facial pressure

Digestive Discomfort

- Frequent bloating and sluggish digestion

- Mucus in your stool

- Acid reflux or heartburn after eating

- Feeling heavy or nauseous after meals

Throat and Mouth Problems

- Sticky, thick saliva that makes swallowing uncomfortable

- Sore throat, even when you're not sick
- Hoarse voice or frequent loss of voice
- Bad breath that won't go away

Other Signs to Watch For

- Feeling constantly tired or foggy-headed
- Ear congestion or frequent ear infections
- Skin breakouts, rashes, or inflammation

Common Causes: Diet, Allergies, and Environmental Factors

Anything that causes inflammation or activates your immune system can change the amount, color or consistency of mucus in different parts of your body. Hormones and genetic conditions can also affect it. Conditions that affect your mucus include:

- **Infections**. Being sick with sinusitis or respiratory infections is the most common cause of excess amounts of thick mucus in your nose or throat.

- **Allergies or irritants**. Allergies and other irritants in your respiratory tract can cause excess clear mucus.

- **Lung diseases**. Damage to your lungs and airways from bronchiectasis, COPD (chronic obstructive pulmonary disease) and other chronic lung diseases can cause mucus buildup.

- **Cystic fibrosis**. CF is a genetic disease that creates thick, sticky mucus that gets stuck in your pancreas and lungs.

- **Digestive issues**. Diverticulitis, inflammatory bowel disease (IBD), irritable bowel syndrome (IBS) and anything that irritates your digestive tract can cause mucus in your poop (stool).

- **Hormone issues**. Menopause and conditions that cause low estrogen decrease the amount of mucus in your reproductive tract, which reduces fertility and causes vaginal dryness.

- **Cancer.** Certain types of cancer can arise from mucin, like mucinous carcinomas.

What You Can Gain From a Mucusless Diet

A mucusless diet is a plant-based diet that focuses on consuming fruits, vegetables, whole grains, beans, nuts, and seeds. The goal is to avoid foods that produce mucus in the body, which can lead to health problems.

The mucusless diet emphasizes the consumption of fruits and vegetables, which are rich in vitamins, minerals, and fiber. These foods can help to improve digestion and reduce inflammation in the body. Whole grains are also an important part of the mucusless diet because they provide complex carbohydrates, which can help to sustain energy levels throughout the day.

It's important to note that the mucusless diet is not a fad diet or a quick fix. It is a long-term lifestyle change that requires dedication and commitment. However, many people who have adopted the mucusless diet have reported significant improvements in their health and well-being.

The History of the Mucusless Diet

The mucusless diet has been around for over a century, but it gained popularity in the early 20th century with the work of Arnold Ehret. Ehret was a health educator and author who believed that the accumulation of mucus in the body was the root cause of many health problems.

Ehret's work was controversial at the time, but it eventually gained a following among health enthusiasts and natural health practitioners. Since then, many other health experts and authors have written about the benefits of the mucusless diet and its potential to improve health and well-being.

How Does a Mucusless Diet Work?

A mucusless diet works by eliminating mucus-forming foods from one's diet and focusing on plant-based foods. By doing so, the body is better able to digest food, which can reduce inflammation and improve gut health.

Plant-based foods are also rich in essential vitamins and minerals that the body needs to function properly. By consuming a diet that is rich in plant-based foods, individuals may experience increased energy levels, improved digestion, and an enhanced immune system.

It's important to note that the mucusless diet is not a one-size-fits-all approach. Every person's body is unique, and what works for one person may not work for another. It's important to consult with a healthcare professional before making any significant changes to your diet.

The mucusless diet is a plant-based dietary philosophy that emphasizes the consumption of fruits, vegetables, whole grains, beans, nuts, and seeds. By eliminating mucus-forming foods from one's diet, individuals may experience improved digestion, reduced inflammation, and an enhanced immune system. While the mucusless diet may not be for everyone, it is a long-term lifestyle change that has the potential to improve health and well-being.

The Benefits of a Mucusless Diet

The mucusless diet offers several benefits for those who follow it. These include improved digestion, enhanced immune system function, increased energy levels, weight loss, and reduced inflammation and allergies.

Improved Digestion and Gut Health

Many people experience digestive issues such as bloating, constipation, and gas, which can be alleviated by following a mucusless diet. The consumption of plant-based foods can help to improve gut health and digestion, which can lead to a reduction in these symptoms.

Furthermore, a mucusless diet can also help to prevent and treat gastrointestinal disorders such as irritable bowel syndrome (IBS), Crohn's disease, and ulcerative colitis. These conditions can cause discomfort and pain, but a mucusless diet can help to reduce inflammation in the gut and promote healing.

Enhanced Immune System Function

The mucusless diet is rich in essential vitamins and minerals that are critical for the immune system. By consuming a diet that is rich in these nutrients, individuals may experience an enhanced immune system function, which can help to ward off illnesses and promote overall health and wellness.

Moreover, a mucusless diet can also help to prevent chronic diseases such as cancer, heart disease, and diabetes. These diseases are often caused by a combination of genetic and lifestyle factors, and a mucusless diet can help to reduce the risk of developing them.

Increased Energy Levels

The mucusless diet is rich in complex carbohydrates, which provide sustained energy throughout the day. By consuming a diet that is rich in these foods, individuals may experience increased energy levels and improved performance, both physically and mentally.

In addition, a mucusless diet can also help to improve sleep quality. This is because plant-based foods contain sleep-promoting nutrients such as magnesium and tryptophan, which can help individuals to fall asleep faster and stay asleep longer.

Weight Loss and Maintenance

The consumption of a mucusless diet can lead to weight loss and maintenance, as a plant-based diet is typically lower in calories and fat than diets that include mucus-forming foods. Additionally, the consumption of a plant-based diet can help to promote satiety, which can lead to a reduction in overeating and snacking.

Moreover, a mucusless diet can also help to reduce the risk of obesity and related conditions such as high blood pressure and high cholesterol. These conditions can increase the risk of heart disease and stroke, but a mucusless diet can help to prevent and manage them.

Reduced Inflammation and Allergies

The consumption of a mucusless diet can help to reduce inflammation and allergies in the body. This is because plant-based foods are typically anti-inflammatory and can help to reduce the production of histamines, which are responsible for many allergy symptoms.

In addition, a mucusless diet can also help to alleviate skin conditions such as eczema and psoriasis. These conditions are often caused by inflammation in the body, and a mucusless diet can help to reduce this inflammation and promote healing.

2
TOP AND WORST FOODS FOR MUCUS CLEANSING

The mucusless diet is a plant-based diet that focuses on consuming foods that are rich in essential vitamins, minerals, and fiber. This type of diet is believed to promote overall health and wellness by reducing the amount of mucus-producing foods that are consumed. Here are some foods that are ideal for a mucusless diet:

Fruits and Vegetables

Fruits and vegetables are the foundation of a mucusless diet. These foods are not only rich in vitamins, minerals, and antioxidants, but they are also low in calories and high in fiber. This means that they can help to promote healthy digestion and weight loss. Some examples of fruits and vegetables that are ideal for a mucusless diet include:

• Berries: These are packed with antioxidants and are a great source of fiber.

• Leafy Greens: These are rich in iron, calcium, and other essential vitamins and minerals.

• Citrus Fruits: These are high in vitamin C, which can help to boost the immune system.

• Cruciferous Vegetables: These include broccoli, cauliflower, and Brussels sprouts, which are rich in fiber and other essential nutrients.

Whole Grains

Whole grains are an important part of the mucusless diet, as they provide complex carbohydrates, fiber, and essential vitamins and minerals. These are some examples of whole grains that are ideal for a mucusless diet:

- Brown Rice: This is a great source of fiber, protein, and essential vitamins and minerals.

- Quinoa: This is a complete protein and is rich in fiber, iron, and other essential nutrients.

- Oats: These are rich in fiber and can help to lower cholesterol levels.

- Barley: This is a great source of fiber and can help to regulate blood sugar levels.

Nuts and Seeds

Nuts and seeds are a great source of healthy fats, protein, and essential vitamins and minerals. These are some examples of nuts and seeds that are ideal for a mucusless diet:

- Almonds: These are rich in vitamin E and can help to lower cholesterol levels.

- Cashews: These are a good source of magnesium, which can help to regulate blood pressure.

• Chia Seeds: These are a great source of omega-3 fatty acids and can help to reduce inflammation.

• Flaxseeds: These are a great source of fiber and can help to lower cholesterol levels.

Plant-Based Protein Sources

Plant-based protein sources are a great alternative to meat and dairy products, which are mucus-forming foods. These are some examples of plant-based protein sources that are ideal for a mucusless diet:

• Legumes: These include beans, lentils, and chickpeas, which are a great source of protein and fiber.

• Tofu: This is a great source of protein and can be used in a variety of dishes.

• Tempeh: This is a fermented soy product that is high in protein and probiotics.

• Seitan: This is a wheat-based protein that is high in protein and low in fat.

By incorporating these foods into your diet, you can help to promote overall health and wellness while reducing the amount of mucus-producing foods that you consume.

Common Hydration and Herbal Remedies for Mucus Reduction

Some home remedies to remove mucus from the lungs naturally include:

1. Lemon juice and honey

Lemon juice and honey contain expectorant action as this combination is rich in vitamin C and antioxidants. It can help to decrease respiratory airway inflammation, which can relieve coughing and speed up cold and flu recovery. In addition, honey can moisten the groat and reduce tissue irritation, which contributes to cough relief.

Ingredients

- Juice of 1 lemon

- 1 tablespoon of honey

- 200 mL (7 oz) of water

How to prepare

Stir the water and lemon juice Ingredients and sweeten with honey before drinking, making sure to drink as soon as possible.

2. Orange, pineapple and watercress juice

Orange, pineapple and watercress juice are rich in vitamin C, vitamin A, iron, potassium and bromelain. These substances contain expectorant, anti-inflammatory and antioxidant action, which help to get rid of mucus and strengthen the immune system to speed-up cold and flu recovery.

Ingredients

- ½ teacup full of watercress leaves and stems

- Juice from 1 orange

- 1 slice of pineapple

How to prepare

Place all the Ingredients in a blender and mix until well-combined. Drink half a cup of this juice 2 to 3 times per day or whenever you have an intense coughing flare-up.

3. Ginger syrup with cinnamon

Ginger syrup with cinnamon contains a drying effect that acts on the respiratory tract lining, making it a great natural expectorant. It can be used to combat coughs with mucus that are caused by the cold or flu.

Ingredients

- 1 cinnamon stick or 1 teaspoon of cinnamon powder

- 1 teacup of peeled ginger root, sliced

- 85 g of brown sugar (demerara or coconut)

- 100 mL (3.5 oz) of water

How to prepare

Boil the water with sugar, making sure to keep stirring until the sugar as completely dissolved. Turn off the stove, add the ginger and cinnamon, and stir. Store the syrup in a clean and dry glass jar. Take 1 teaspoon of ginger syrup 3 times per day.

This syrup should not be used by people with a history of clotting problems or by people who take anticoagulants, as it can increase your risk for bleeding and bruising. In addition, this syrup should not be used by pregnant women who are close to their due date or with a history of miscarriages.

4. Peppermint tea

Peppermint tea is rich in menthol, an essential oil that can improve symptoms like coughing, mucus, runny nose, stuffy nose and headache, all which are common with the cold and flu.

This tea also contains antibacterial, antiviral and anti-inflammatory properties, which help the body to fight a cold and recover quicker.

Ingredients

- 6 leaves of chopped mint leaves

- 150 mL (5 oz) of boiling water

How to prepare

Add the mint to a teacup with the boiling water and allow to soak for 5 to 10 minutes. Strain, sweeten with honey if desired, and take 3 to 4 cups per day.

5. Thyme and honey infusion

This thyme and honey infusion is rich in anti-inflammatory and antiseptic substances, like thymol, carvacrol, cymene and linalool. These contain expectorant action, which helps with the elimination of mucus from the lungs, and they additionally help to lubricate the throat to relieve coughing, runny nose and stuffy nose.

People with an allergy to honey, propolis or pollen should not add honey to this infusion and should only take it with thyme.

Ingredients

- 1 tablespoon of dried thyme extract or 2 branches of fresh thyme

- 1 liter (about 4 cups) of boiling water

- 1 tablespoon of honey

How to prepare

Add the dry thyme to the boiling water and allow to soak for 5 to 10 minutes. Strain and drink 3 cups per day.

Thyme infusions should not be used by people with stomach problems (like gastritis or ulcers), with liver disease, or by those who take anticoagulants, like warfarin or clopidogrel.

6. Onion and garlic syrup

This home remedy for mucus in the lungs is made with onion and garlic, which contains expectorant and antiseptic properties. It helps to loosen phlegm, strengthen the immune system and reduce lung inflammation to prevent more mucus production.

Ingredients

- 1 medium onion, grated

- 1 smashed clove of garlic

- Honey

How to prepare

Place the onion and garlic in a glass container and add enough honey to cover the onion and garlic. Mix all the Ingredients and store in the refrigerator for one day. Children over 2 can take 2.5 mL of syrup, or about half a teaspoon, 3 times per day. Adults can take 5 mL or 1 teaspoon, up to 3 times per day. Discard any unused syrup after 1 week in the fridge.

Because it contains honey, this onion and garlic syrup should not be used in children under the age of 2, nor by pregnant women with gestational diabetes. People with a history of diabetes should also avoid taking this syrup, as the honey can cause sugar spikes.

7. Eucalyptus vapor inhalation

A great way to treat coughing and mucus in the lungs is to inhale vapor infused with eucalyptus. It contains expectorant and anti-septic properties, which help to quickly relieve nasal congestion.

Some people may be sensitive to eucalyptus essential oil, however, and therefore they may actually experience a worsening in symptoms. If you notice your symptoms worsening with this inhalation, discontinue use immediately.

Ingredients

- 5 drops of eucalyptus essential oil

- 1 liter (about 4 cups) of boiling water

How to prepare

Place the boiling water in a bowel and add the drops of eucalyptus essential oil. Then cover your head and the bowl with a towel and inhale the vapor. Try leaning your head toward the bowl and inhaling as deeply as possible for 10 minutes. You can repeat this 2 to 3 times per day. The towel helps to make the vapor last for longer.

If you do not have this essential oil at home, you can use fresh eucalyptus leaves and soak them in the boiling water. The natural oils contained in the leaves will be released in the water vapor.

8. ~~Licorice tea~~ CKD

Licorice tea, prepared with the medicinal plant Glycyrrhiza glabra is rich in substances like glycyrrhizin, glabridin, apigenin and liquiritin. It contains potent expectorant action as well as antioxidant, antibacterial and anti-inflammatory properties that help to fight phlegm and other respiratory problems, like a cold or bronchitis.

Ingredients

- 1 teaspoon of licorice root

- 1 teacup of boiling water

- Honey to sweeten to taste

How to prepare

Add the licorice to the cup of boiling water, cover, and allow to soak for 10 minutes. Strain and sweeten with honey if desired. Drink this tea up to twice per day.

Licorice root should not be consumed by pregnant or breastfeeding women or by people with a history of cardiac problems, renal disease or low potassium.

9. Guaco and mallow tea

Guaco and mallow tea have a soothing effect on the bronchi, which reduced the production of phlegm as well as any shortness of breath. In addition, the properties found in guaco can make mucus thinner, which helps to eliminate it from the throat and lungs.

Ingredients

- 1 teaspoon of dried mallow flowers or leaves
- 1 tablespoon of fresh guaco leaves
- 1 cup of boiling water

How to prepare

Place the mallow and guaco in the cup of boiling water. Cover for about 10 minutes, then strain and drink. The recommended dose for adults is one cup up to 3 times per day.

This tea should only be taken in those over the age of 2. Younger children will benefit from water vapor inhalations.

10. Butcher's-broom tea

Butcher's-broom tea, prepared with the medicinal plant Scoparia dulcis, is rich in fatty acids, diterpenes, and flavonoids with anti-inflammatory, antioxidant, expectorant and antiseptic properties. These help to relieve coughs from colds, asthma and bronchitis.

Ingredients

- 10 g of butcher's-broom

- 500 mL (2 cups) of water

How to prepare

Place the butcher's-broom and the water in a pot and boil for 10 minutes. Then allow to cool, strain, and drink 3 to 4 cups per day.

Butcher's-broom should not be used by pregnant women as it is associated with increased risk for miscarriage. This plant should also not be used during breastfeeding.

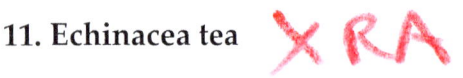

11. Echinacea tea

Echinacea tea is rich in antioxidant, anti-inflammatory and immuno-stimulating substances, like flavonoids, chicory aids, and rosmarinic. These help to strengthen the immune system and reduce the duration of colds, the flu or sinusitis, which help to relieve phlegmy coughs.

Ingredients

- 1 teaspoon of echinacea root or leaves

- 1 cup of boiling water

How to prepare

Place 1 teaspoon of echinacea root or leaves into the cup of boiling water. Allow to soak for 15 minutes, strain, then drink twice a day.

Echinacea tea should be used by children, pregnant women, or breastfeeding women. It should also be avoided in people with a history of asthma, tuberculosis, or autoimmune diseases, like rheumatoid arthritis, lupus or psoriasis.

To complement these home remedies, you should drink plenty of water to help thin out very thick phlegm.

The Worst Offenders: Dairy, Processed Foods, and Sugar

The following secondary, denaturalized, or inorganic food substances are harmful and mucus-forming foods and should be eliminated from the diet.

Salt: For those who are accustomed to large amounts of salt, this may sound difficult but if you will substitute coarsely ground pepper and savory herbs, and adding powdered kelp, you will find that the craving for salt will immediately disappear.

The black pepper is a good nutritional herb and helps rebuild the body when used in its natural state. But when pepper is cooked in food, the molecular structure changes, so it becomes an inorganic irritant (high heat changes the cayenne, black pepper and spices from organics to inorganic), and this is the only time that damage results.

The use of salts that are of a vegetable or potassium base (such as Dr. Jensen's, Dr. Bronner's and other various ones, which in some cases contain sea salt) is all right, providing it is not overdone.

Eggs: No eggs should be eaten in any form.

Sugar: Sugar and all sugar products should be eliminated. You may use honey, sorghum molasses or blackstrap molasses, but no refined sugar of any type.

Meat: Eliminate all red meats from the diet. A little white fish once a week, or a bit of young chicken that has not been fed commercial food or inoculated with formaldehyde and other anti-spoilage serums, would be all right (as these are higher forms of edible flesh), but do not use them too often.

Milk: Eliminate all dairy products – which include butter, cheese, cottage cheese, milk, yogurt (especially butter), you can train your taste buds to like and enjoy a good, fresh, bland olive oil on vegetables and salads and you will discover this to be one of the choicest foods there is.

Flour and Flour Products: The reason that this is eliminated is that flour, when heated and baked at high temperatures, changes to a mucous-forming substance.

This is no longer a food, which means it has no life remaining therein. All wholesome food is organic, where unwholesome food or dead food is inorganic. This is the key to our whole mucusless program.

How to Identify Mucus-Forming Foods

1. Foods high in histamines

Foods that cause your body to release histamine can increase mucus production. However, this often only affects people who have histamine sensitivity or intolerance, which is likely to be the result of enzyme deficits in the gut. Foods high in histamines include:

• Some types of fish, such as tuna, pike, and mackerel

• Processed meats

• Mayonnaise

• Dairy products such as milk, cheese, butter, and cream (for some people)

- Fermented products such as alcohol, yogurt, and sauerkraut

- Spinach

- Tomatoes

- Citrus fruits

- Grapes

- Bananas

- Strawberries

2. Processed foods

Food additives such as preservatives and thickeners can mess with your gut and cause problems such as dangerous inflammatory reactions or intestinal disease. Both excessive and inadequate mucus production can be triggered by these artificial substances.

3. Chocolate

Chocolate can also contribute to increased mucus production, particularly if you have an acid reflux disorder such as laryngopharyngeal reflux or gastroesophageal reflux disease (GERD). Chocolate can weaken your lower and upper esophageal sphincters. These sphincters serve as gatekeepers that make sure that food and liquids flow in the proper direction (downward) and prevent stomach acid from entering your pharynx, larynx, or esophagus. You can get hoarseness, a sore throat, heartburn, a persistent cough and mucus in the back of your throat if the sphincters are weak and stomach acid gets into the wrong places.

4. Coffee

Caffeine is another chemical that can weaken your esophageal sphincters and cause stomach acid to back up into your esophagus and throat. Phlegm production may result from this irritation.

5. Alcohol

Alcohol can weaken the esophageal sphincters, creating irritation and increased phlegm, just like other foods and beverages that cause mucus. Alcohol is also a diuretic, which means that if you consume too much alcohol, it could lead to dehydration and make it difficult for phlegm to drain properly.

6. Carbonated beverages

If you have a recurrent phlegm issue, carbonated beverages may be worsening the problem. Carbonation drinks are full of gas, and more gas can lead to irritation and associated phlegm.

7. Foods that trigger reflux

According to studies, foods that trigger GERD can also increase mucus production:

• Fried food

• Chilis

• Tomatoes

• Citrus fruits

• Peppermint

• Fatty meats such as bacon

- Cheese

3
DELICIOUS MUCUSLESS BREAKFAST RECIPES TO TRY

1. Mucusless Alkaline Green Smoothie

Calories: 250 kcal | **Protein**: 4g | **Carbs**: 45g | **Fats**: 6g

Ingredients:

- 2 cups kale or spinach
- 1 ripe banana
- 1 cup coconut water
- 1 tbsp flaxseeds
- ½ tsp ginger (anti-inflammatory)

- ½ avocado (for creaminess)

Instructions:

1. Blend all ingredients until smooth.

2. Pour into a glass and enjoy immediately.

2. Chia Seed Pudding with Berries

Calories: 280 kcal | **Protein**: 6g | **Carbs**: 38g | **Fats**: 12g

Ingredients:

- 3 tbsp chia seeds
- 1 cup almond milk (unsweetened)
- 1 tsp maple syrup
- ½ cup mixed berries (strawberries, blueberries, raspberries)
- 1 tbsp shredded coconut

Instructions:

1. Mix chia seeds, almond milk, and maple syrup in a jar.

2. Let it sit overnight to thicken.

3. Top with berries and coconut before serving.

3. Quinoa Porridge with Cinnamon

Calories: 320 kcal | **Protein**: 8g | **Carbs**: 55g | **Fats**: 6g

Ingredients:

- ½ cup quinoa
- 1 cup water
- ½ tsp cinnamon
- 1 tbsp chopped walnuts
- 1 tbsp raisins

- 1 tsp date syrup

Instructions:

1. Cook quinoa in water until soft.
2. Stir in cinnamon, walnuts, and raisins.
3. Drizzle with date syrup and serve warm.

4. Alkaline Fruit Salad

Calories: 210 kcal | **Protein**: 3g | **Carbs**: 48g | **Fats**: 1g

Ingredients:

- 1 cup papaya
- ½ cup pineapple
- 1 kiwi
- ½ cup watermelon
- 1 tbsp lime juice

Instructions:

1. Chop all fruits and mix in a bowl.
2. Drizzle with lime juice and serve fresh.

5. Sprouted Buckwheat Granola

Calories: 350 kcal | **Protein**: 10g | **Carbs**: 50g | **Fats**: 12g

Ingredients:

- ½ cup sprouted buckwheat
- ¼ cup pumpkin seeds
- ¼ cup dried figs
- 1 tbsp coconut flakes
- 1 tsp cinnamon

Instructions:

1. Mix all ingredients and store in an airtight container.

2. Serve with almond milk.

6. Coconut Yogurt with Flaxseeds

Calories: 290 kcal | **Protein**: 5g | **Carbs**: 30g | **Fats**: 15g

Ingredients:

- 1 cup unsweetened coconut yogurt
- 1 tbsp flaxseeds
- ½ cup fresh berries
- 1 tsp agave syrup

Instructions:

1. Mix ingredients in a bowl and enjoy.

7. Avocado Toast on Spelt Bread

Calories: 320 kcal | **Protein**: 8g | **Carbs**: 40g | **Fats**: 15g

Ingredients:

- 1 slice spelt bread
- ½ avocado, mashed
- 1 tsp lemon juice
- ¼ tsp cayenne pepper

Instructions:

1. Spread avocado on toast, drizzle lemon juice, and sprinkle cayenne pepper.

8. Warm Fig & Date Smoothie

Calories: 280 kcal | **Protein**: 4g | **Carbs**: 50g | **Fats**: 6g

Ingredients:

- 3 dried figs
- 2 dates
- 1 cup warm almond milk
- ½ tsp cinnamon

Instructions:

1. Blend until smooth and enjoy warm.

9. Sautéed Plantains with Walnuts

Calories: 350 kcal | **Protein**: 6g | **Carbs**: 50g | **Fats**: 14g

Ingredients:

- 1 ripe plantain, sliced
- 1 tbsp coconut oil
- ¼ cup walnuts

Instructions:

1. Sauté plantains in coconut oil until golden.

2. Top with walnuts and serve warm.

10. Sweet Potato Pancakes

Calories: 340 kcal | **Protein**: 7g | **Carbs**: 60g | **Fats**: 7g

Ingredients:

- ½ cup mashed sweet potato
- ½ cup spelt flour
- 1 tsp baking soda
- 1 tsp cinnamon
- ½ cup almond milk

Instructions:

1. Mix ingredients and cook pancakes on a non-stick pan.

11. Apple-Cinnamon Breakfast Bowl

Calories: 290 kcal | **Protein**: 5g | **Carbs**: 50g | **Fats**: 6g

Ingredients:

- 1 apple, chopped
- ½ cup cooked millet
- ½ tsp cinnamon
- 1 tbsp pumpkin seeds

Instructions:

1. Mix and serve warm.

12. Mango-Banana Smoothie Bowl

Calories: 280 kcal | **Protein**: 4g | **Carbs**: 50g | **Fats**: 5g

Ingredients:

- 1 ripe banana
- 1 cup mango chunks
- ½ cup coconut milk

Instructions:

1. Blend and top with coconut flakes.

13. Amaranth Porridge with Dates

Calories: 320 kcal | **Protein**: 7g | **Carbs**: 55g | **Fats**: 6g

Ingredients:

- ½ cup cooked amaranth
- 3 chopped dates
- 1 cup warm almond milk

Instructions:

1. Mix and serve warm.

14. Cucumber & Avocado Wrap

Calories: 300 kcal | **Protein**: 6g | **Carbs**: 40g | **Fats**: 12g

Ingredients:

- 1 spelt tortilla
- ½ avocado
- ½ cucumber, sliced

Instructions:

1. Fill tortilla with avocado and cucumber.

15. Pineapple-Ginger Detox Juice

Calories: 180 kcal | **Protein**: 2g | **Carbs**: 45g | **Fats**: 0g

Ingredients:

- 1 cup pineapple chunks
- 1 inch ginger
- 1 cup coconut water

Instructions:

1. Blend and drink fresh.

4

DELICIOUS MUCUSLESS LUNCH RECIPES TO TRY

1. Quinoa & Roasted Veggie Bowl

Calories: 380 kcal | **Protein**: 12g | **Carbs**: 55g | **Fats**: 12g

Ingredients:

- 1 cup cooked quinoa
- ½ cup roasted zucchini
- ½ cup roasted bell peppers
- ½ cup cherry tomatoes
- 1 tbsp olive oil

- 1 tsp lemon juice
- 1 tsp dried oregano

Instructions:

1. Toss cooked quinoa with roasted vegetables.
2. Drizzle with olive oil, lemon juice, and oregano.
3. Serve warm.

2. Avocado & Cucumber Wrap

Calories: 320 kcal | **Protein**: 7g | **Carbs**: 45g | **Fats**: 15g

Ingredients:

- 1 spelt tortilla
- ½ avocado, mashed
- ½ cucumber, sliced
- 1 tbsp hemp seeds

- 1 tsp lime juice

Instructions:

1. Spread mashed avocado on the tortilla.
2. Add cucumber slices and hemp seeds.
3. Roll and enjoy.

3. Sweet Potato & Lentil Stew

Calories: 400 kcal | **Protein**: 14g | **Carbs**: 65g | **Fats**: 7g

Ingredients:

- 1 medium sweet potato, diced
- ½ cup cooked lentils
- 1 cup vegetable broth
- ½ tsp cumin

- ½ tsp turmeric

Instructions:

1. Simmer all ingredients in a pot for 15 minutes.
2. Serve warm.

4. Mango & Spinach Salad

Calories: 270 kcal I **Protein**: 6g I **Carbs**: 40g I **Fats**: 10g

Ingredients:

- 2 cups fresh spinach
- 1 ripe mango, sliced
- ¼ cup walnuts
- 1 tbsp balsamic vinegar

Instructions:

1. Toss all ingredients together.

2. Serve fresh.

5. Spaghetti Squash & Pesto

Calories: 350 kcal | **Protein**: 10g | **Carbs**: 50g | **Fats**: 14g

Ingredients:

- 1 cup roasted spaghetti squash
- 2 tbsp homemade basil pesto (basil, olive oil, garlic, walnuts)

Instructions:

1. Mix roasted spaghetti squash with pesto.
2. Serve warm.

6. Chickpea & Avocado Salad

Calories: 340 kcal | **Protein**: 12g | **Carbs**: 40g | **Fats**: 15g

Ingredients:

- ½ cup cooked chickpeas
- ½ avocado, diced
- ½ red onion, chopped
- 1 tbsp lemon juice

Instructions:

1. Toss all ingredients together.
2. Serve chilled.

7. Baked Plantain with Black Beans

Calories: 420 kcal | **Protein**: 15g | **Carbs**: 70g | **Fats**: 8g

Ingredients:

- 1 ripe plantain, sliced
- ½ cup black beans
- 1 tbsp olive oil

Instructions:

1. Bake plantain slices at 375°F for 20 minutes.
2. Serve with black beans.

8. Roasted Cauliflower & Tahini Dressing

Calories: 310 kcal | **Protein**: 9g | **Carbs**: 30g | **Fats**: 15g

Ingredients:

- 1 cup roasted cauliflower
- 1 tbsp tahini
- 1 tsp lemon juice

Instructions:

1. Drizzle roasted cauliflower with tahini dressing.
2. Serve warm.

9. Stuffed Bell Peppers with Quinoa

Calories: 390 kcal | **Protein**: 14g | **Carbs**: 60g | **Fats**: 9g

Ingredients:

- 2 bell peppers, halved
- 1 cup cooked quinoa

- ½ cup diced tomatoes

Instructions:

1. Stuff bell peppers with quinoa and diced tomatoes.
2. Bake at 375°F for 20 minutes.

10. Cucumber & Avocado Gazpacho

Calories: 280 kcal | **Protein**: 5g | **Carbs**: 40g | **Fats**: 12g

Ingredients:

- 1 cucumber, peeled and chopped
- ½ avocado
- 1 tbsp lime juice
- ½ cup coconut water

Instructions:

1. Blend all ingredients until smooth.
2. Serve chilled.

11. Roasted Eggplant with Tomato Sauce

Calories: 310 kcal | **Protein**: 7g | **Carbs**: 35g | **Fats**: 12g

Ingredients:

- 1 eggplant, sliced
- 1 cup tomato sauce
- 1 tbsp olive oil

Instructions:

1. Roast eggplant at 375°F for 20 minutes.
2. Top with tomato sauce and serve.

12. Zucchini Noodles with Cashew Cream

Calories: 340 kcal | **Protein**: 8g | **Carbs**: 40g | **Fats**: 15g

Ingredients:

- 1 zucchini, spiralized
- 2 tbsp cashew cream (cashews blended with lemon juice and garlic)

Instructions:

1. Toss zucchini noodles with cashew cream.
2. Serve chilled.

13. Carrot & Beet Slaw

Calories: 280 kcal | **Protein**: 5g | **Carbs**: 45g | **Fats**: 8g

Ingredients:

- 1 cup shredded carrots

- ½ cup shredded beets
- 1 tbsp apple cider vinegar

Instructions:

1. Toss all ingredients together.
2. Serve fresh.

14. Steamed Kale & Garlic Mushrooms

Calories: 290 kcal | **Protein**: 10g | **Carbs**: 30g | **Fats**: 12g

Ingredients:

- 2 cups steamed kale
- 1 cup sautéed mushrooms
- 1 tbsp olive oil

Instructions:

1. Sauté mushrooms with olive oil and serve over steamed kale.

15. Pineapple & Avocado Salsa with Quinoa

Calories: 350 kcal | **Protein**: 9g | **Carbs**: 50g | **Fats**: 12g

Ingredients:

- ½ cup diced pineapple
- ½ avocado, diced
- 1 cup cooked quinoa
- 1 tbsp lime juice

Instructions:

1. Toss all ingredients together.
2. Serve fresh.

5
DELICIOUS MUCUSLESS DINNER RECIPES TO TRY

1. Roasted Eggplant & Quinoa Bowl

Calories: 380 kcal | **Protein**: 12g | **Carbs**: 55g | **Fats**: 10g

Ingredients:

- 1 medium eggplant, sliced
- 1 cup cooked quinoa
- ½ tsp cumin
- 1 tbsp olive oil
- 1 tbsp chopped parsley

Instructions:

1. Roast eggplant slices at 400°F for 20 minutes.

2. Toss with cooked quinoa, cumin, olive oil, and parsley.

2. Zucchini Noodles with Avocado Pesto

Calories: 320 kcal | **Protein**: 8g | **Carbs**: 30g | **Fats**: 18g

Ingredients:

- 2 zucchinis, spiralized
- ½ avocado
- ¼ cup fresh basil
- 1 tbsp olive oil
- 1 clove garlic

Instructions:

1. Blend avocado, basil, olive oil, and garlic into a creamy pesto.

2. Toss with zucchini noodles and serve.

3. Stuffed Bell Peppers with Lentils

Calories: 410 kcal | **Protein**: 18g | **Carbs**: 55g | **Fats**: 10g

Ingredients:

- 2 bell peppers, halved
- 1 cup cooked lentils
- ½ cup diced tomatoes
- 1 tsp smoked paprika

Instructions:

1. Stuff bell peppers with lentils, tomatoes, and paprika.

2. Bake at 375°F for 25 minutes.

4. Cauliflower & Chickpea Curry

Calories: 390 kcal | **Protein**: 14g | **Carbs**: 50g | **Fats**: 14g

Ingredients:

- 1 cup cauliflower florets
- ½ cup cooked chickpeas
- 1 tsp turmeric
- 1 cup coconut milk

Instructions:

1. Sauté cauliflower and chickpeas with turmeric.
2. Add coconut milk and simmer for 15 minutes.

5. Sweet Potato & Kale Stir-Fry

Calories: 370 kcal | **Protein**: 10g | **Carbs**: 60g | **Fats**: 9g

Ingredients:

- 1 medium sweet potato, diced
- 1 cup kale, chopped
- 1 tbsp coconut oil
- ½ tsp garlic powder

Instructions:

1. Sauté sweet potato in coconut oil until tender.
2. Add kale and garlic powder, stir-frying for 3 minutes.

6. Spaghetti Squash & Mushroom Medley

Calories: 340 kcal | **Protein**: 9g | **Carbs**: 50g | **Fats**: 10g

Ingredients:

- 1 cup roasted spaghetti squash
- ½ cup mushrooms, sliced
- 1 tbsp olive oil
- ½ tsp thyme

Instructions:

1. Roast spaghetti squash at 375°F for 40 minutes.
2. Sauté mushrooms with olive oil and thyme.
3. Toss together and serve.

7. Broccoli & Almond Stir-Fry

Calories: 350 kcal | **Protein**: 12g | **Carbs**: 40g | **Fats**: 15g

Ingredients:

- 1 cup broccoli florets
- ¼ cup almonds
- 1 tbsp sesame oil
- 1 tsp tamari

Instructions:

1. Stir-fry broccoli and almonds in sesame oil.
2. Add tamari and serve warm.

8. Warm Lentil & Spinach Salad

Calories: 380 kcal | **Protein**: 16g | **Carbs**: 50g | **Fats**: 10g

Ingredients:

- 1 cup cooked lentils
- 2 cups fresh spinach
- 1 tbsp balsamic vinegar
- 1 tbsp chopped walnuts

Instructions:

1. Toss warm lentils with spinach, vinegar, and walnuts.

9. Roasted Carrot & Ginger Soup

Calories: 300 kcal | **Protein**: 7g | **Carbs**: 45g | **Fats**: 9g

Ingredients:

- 2 large carrots, roasted
- 1 inch ginger, grated
- 2 cups vegetable broth

Instructions:

1. Blend roasted carrots, ginger, and broth until smooth.
2. Heat and serve warm.

10. Butternut Squash & Quinoa Pilaf

Calories: 400 kcal | **Protein**: 12g | **Carbs**: 60g | **Fats**: 10g

Ingredients:

- 1 cup cooked quinoa

- 1 cup roasted butternut squash
- 1 tbsp pumpkin seeds

Instructions:

1. Toss quinoa with roasted squash and pumpkin seeds.

11. Cabbage & Avocado Wraps

Calories: 320 kcal | **Protein**: 8g | **Carbs**: 35g | **Fats**: 15g

Ingredients:

- 3 large cabbage leaves
- ½ avocado, mashed
- ½ cup shredded carrots

Instructions:

1. Spread avocado inside cabbage leaves.

2. Fill with carrots and roll into wraps.

12. Grilled Asparagus & Quinoa Salad

Calories: 370 kcal | **Protein**: 14g | **Carbs**: 50g | **Fats**: 10g

Ingredients:

- 1 cup cooked quinoa
- 1 cup grilled asparagus
- 1 tbsp lemon juice

Instructions:

1. Toss quinoa with grilled asparagus and lemon juice.

13. Baked Cauliflower Steaks

Calories: 330 kcal | **Protein**: 10g | **Carbs**: 35g | **Fats**: 12g

Ingredients:

- 2 thick slices cauliflower
- 1 tbsp olive oil
- ½ tsp smoked paprika

Instructions:

1. Bake cauliflower steaks at 400°F for 20 minutes.

14. Roasted Brussels Sprouts & Walnuts

Calories: 350 kcal | **Protein**: 10g | **Carbs**: 40g | **Fats**: 14g

Ingredients:

- 1 cup Brussels sprouts, halved
- ¼ cup walnuts
- 1 tbsp balsamic vinegar

Instructions:

1. Roast Brussels sprouts at 375°F for 25 minutes.
2. Toss with walnuts and balsamic vinegar.

15. Steamed Okra & Tomato Salad

Calories: 290 kcal | **Protein**: 6g | **Carbs**: 40g | **Fats**: 8g

Ingredients:

- 1 cup okra, steamed
- ½ cup cherry tomatoes, halved
- 1 tbsp lemon juice

Instructions:

1. Toss steamed okra with cherry tomatoes and lemon juice.

6

DELICIOUS MUCUSLESS SNACK AND DESSERT RECIPES TO TRY

1. Alkaline Energy Balls

Calories: 180 kcal | **Protein**: 5g | **Carbs**: 25g | **Fats**: 8g

Ingredients:

- ½ cup raw almonds
- ½ cup dates, pitted
- 1 tbsp chia seeds
- 1 tbsp shredded coconut
- 1 tsp cinnamon

Instructions:

1. Blend all ingredients until sticky.
2. Roll into small balls and refrigerate for 30 minutes.

2. Cucumber & Avocado Slices

Calories: 150 kcal | **Protein**: 3g | **Carbs**: 10g | **Fats**: 10g

Ingredients:

- ½ avocado, sliced
- ½ cucumber, sliced
- 1 tsp lemon juice

Instructions:

1. Place avocado slices on cucumber rounds.
2. Drizzle with lemon juice and serve.

3. Mango & Coconut Chia Pudding

Calories: 220 kcal | **Protein**: 6g | **Carbs**: 35g | **Fats**: 9g

Ingredients:

- ½ cup coconut milk
- 2 tbsp chia seeds
- ½ cup mango chunks

Instructions:

1. Mix coconut milk and chia seeds, let sit for 1 hour.
2. Top with mango and enjoy.

4. Spiced Roasted Chickpeas

Calories: 200 kcal | **Protein**: 8g | **Carbs**: 30g | **Fats**: 5g

Ingredients:

- ½ cup cooked chickpeas
- ½ tsp cumin
- ½ tsp paprika

Instructions:

1. Toss chickpeas with spices and roast at 375°F for 15 minutes.

5. Watermelon & Mint Salad

Calories: 120 kcal | **Protein**: 2g | **Carbs**: 30g | **Fats**: 0g

Ingredients:

- 1 cup watermelon, cubed

- 1 tbsp fresh mint, chopped

Instructions:

1. Mix watermelon cubes with mint and chill before serving.

6. Almond Butter & Banana Bites

Calories: 190 kcal | **Protein**: 5g | **Carbs**: 28g | **Fats**: 7g

Ingredients:

- 1 banana, sliced
- 1 tbsp almond butter

Instructions:

1. Spread almond butter on banana slices and enjoy.

7. Baked Plantain Chips

Calories: 180 kcal | **Protein**: 2g | **Carbs**: 40g | **Fats**: 2g

Ingredients:

- 1 ripe plantain, thinly sliced
- 1 tsp olive oil

Instructions:

1. Toss plantain slices with olive oil and bake at 375°F for 15 minutes.

8. Apple & Walnut Snack

Calories: 200 kcal | **Protein**: 4g | **Carbs**: 28g | **Fats**: 10g

Ingredients:

- 1 apple, sliced
- ¼ cup walnuts

Instructions:

1. Mix apple slices with walnuts and enjoy.

9. Carrot & Hummus Sticks

Calories: 180 kcal | **Protein**: 6g | **Carbs**: 25g | **Fats**: 8g

Ingredients:

- 1 carrot, cut into sticks
- ¼ cup hummus

Instructions:

1. Dip carrot sticks into hummus and enjoy.

10. Pineapple & Coconut Bites

Calories: 170 kcal | **Protein**: 2g | **Carbs**: 35g | **Fats**: 3g

Ingredients:

- ½ cup pineapple chunks
- 1 tbsp shredded coconut

Instructions:

1. Toss pineapple chunks with shredded coconut and serve.

11. Zucchini Chips

Calories: 160 kcal | **Protein**: 3g | **Carbs**: 20g | **Fats**: 7g

Ingredients:

- 1 zucchini, thinly sliced
- 1 tsp olive oil

Instructions:

1. Toss zucchini slices with olive oil and bake at 350°F for 20 minutes.

12. Almond & Fig Snack

Calories: 190 kcal | **Protein**: 6g | **Carbs**: 28g | **Fats**: 7g

Ingredients:

- 4 dried figs
- ¼ cup almonds

Instructions:

1. Pair dried figs with almonds for a simple snack.

13. Fresh Guacamole & Veggie Sticks

Calories: 210 kcal | **Protein**: 4g | **Carbs**: 18g | **Fats**: 14g

Ingredients:

- ½ avocado, mashed
- 1 tsp lime juice
- 1 carrot, sliced

Instructions:

1. Mash avocado with lime juice and serve with carrot sticks.

14. Cantaloupe & Mint Delight

Calories: 130 kcal | **Protein**: 2g | **Carbs**: 30g | **Fats**: 0g

Ingredients:

- 1 cup cantaloupe, cubed
- 1 tbsp fresh mint, chopped

Instructions:

1. Mix cantaloupe cubes with mint and enjoy.

15. Roasted Pumpkin Seeds

Calories: 180 kcal | **Protein**: 7g | **Carbs**: 10g | **Fats**: 14g

Ingredients:

- ¼ cup pumpkin seeds
- ½ tsp sea salt

Instructions:

1. Roast pumpkin seeds at 350°F for 10 minutes and sprinkle with salt.

7
HEALTHY TIPS FOR CLEARING MUCUS

The best way to clear a buildup depends on the underlying cause and contributing factors. Common home care strategies include:

• Using an over-the-counter (OTC) saline nasal spray

• Taking OTC non-drowsy decongestants or antihistamines

• Rubbing a product that contains eucalyptus oil on the chest and throat or inhaling it

• Avoiding all allergens, including those in foods

• Gently pounding or tapping on the back and chest repeatedly to loosen the mucus

- Adding humidity to the air by using a humidifier or taking a warm shower or bath

- Applying a warm, moist washcloth over the face

- Covering the nose with a scarf in cold weather

- Not smoking and avoiding secondhand smoke

Many natural products can reduce mucus buildups or treat the respiratory conditions that cause them. Natural remedies with some scientific backing include:

- Licorice root

- Most berries

- Echinacea

- Ginseng

- Eucalyptus oil

When to contact a doctor

When excessive mucus production or buildups happen with no clear cause, contact a healthcare professional.

Also seek professional care if mucus:

• Is very thick

• Has a color — healthy mucus is clear

• Interferes with breathing

• Does not respond to home treatment

• Lasts longer than a few weeks

Also, talk with a doctor if troublesome mucus occurs with:

• A fever or chills

• Unexplained exhaustion

• Trouble sleeping

• Wheezing or noisy breathing

• Breathing changes, such as rapid, shallow breathing or shortness of breath

• A lack of appetite or weight loss

• Chest pain or pain when breathing

• Pus or blood

• A cough

• Nausea and vomiting

• Acid reflux

• A severe sore throat

• Rash on the chest, throat, or neck

• Bluish or pale coloring of the skin, especially around the fingers, toes, and lips

• Swelling of the throat, neck, head, feet, or ankles

• Confusion or other changes in mental functioning or state

Additional Common Questions

What's the difference between phlegm and mucus?

Phlegm is a type of mucus that you usually cough up from your lower respiratory tract. It's typically thicker than normal mucus because it's helping fight an infection.

Should you swallow phlegm or spit it out?

If you cough up phlegm into your mouth, it won't hurt you to swallow it. Some people find that this makes them cough or it feels like it gets stuck in their throat. Or it just feels gross. In that case, it's perfectly OK to spit out phlegm — as long as you're being considerate of other people while doing it.

If you can, find a tissue or napkin so you can spit your mucus into it and throw it away. Then, be sure to wash your hands. If you don't have a tissue, step away from others before spitting.

Printed in Great Britain
by Amazon